MW01527691

Joseph A. Dandurand

The Rumour

Joehie,

Please enjoy my words...

[signature]

BookLand
press

Copyright © 2018 by Joseph A. Dandurand

All rights reserved. No part of this publication may be reproduced or transmitted in any form or by any means, electronic or mechanical, including photocopying, recording or any information storage and retrieval, without the written permission of the publisher. Names, characters, places and incidents are either the product of the author's imagination or used fictitiously, and any resemblance to actual persons living or dead, events or locales is entirely coincidental. All trademarks are properties of their respective owners.

Published by BookLand Press
15 Allstate Parkway
Suite 600
Markham, Ontario L3R 5B4
www.booklandpress.com

Printed in Canada

Front cover image © Tukkki

Library and Archives Canada Cataloguing in Publication

Dandurand, Joseph A., author
        The rumour / Joseph A. Dandurand.

(Canadian Indigenous voices)
Poems.
Issued in print and electronic formats.
ISBN 978-1-77231-077-1 (softcover).--ISBN 978-1-77231-078-8
(EPUB).--ISBN 978-1-77231-079-5 (PDF)

        I. Title. II. Series: Canadian Indigenous voices

PS8557.A523R85 2018   C811'.54   C2018-901636-1
                                                C2018-901637-X

Canada Council   Conseil des arts
for the Arts   du Canada

ONTARIO ARTS COUNCIL
CONSEIL DES ARTS DE L'ONTARIO
an Ontario government agency
un organisme du gouvernement de l'Ontario

We acknowledge the support of the Canada Council for the Arts, which last year invested $153 million to bring the arts to Canadians throughout the country. We acknowledge the support of the Ontario Arts Council (OAC), an agency of the Government of Ontario. We acknowledge the financial support of the Ontario Media Development Corporation for our publishing activities.

The Rumour

Table of Contents

What we all deny | 7

My confession | 10

A sacred world | 12

We walk together | 14

The rumour | 16

The old days | 18

Am I the one? | 20

Finding the animal | 22

Where we are now | 24

Smile looking down | 26

The glorious rains | 28

Passage to exhale | 30

On the stage of life | 33

Fire from the sky | 36

Late summer moon | 39

Man of the madhouse | 42

A new chapter | 44

A dream | 46

Beating the odds | 48

Perhaps | 50

Acceptance | 52

Let us play | 54

Darkness | 56

One day | 58

The director | 60

I am my own memory | 63

A winter morning | 65

Look at her | 67

The stone circle | 70

Living hell | 73

People trying to sleep | 76

Writing on the wall | 78

What we all deny

I can feel the pain of
those who have fallen
and have gone toward
the light that we all
look forward to going
to one day

I can taste the precious
sweetness of love as
it gathers at my feet
and I walk through it
like fallen leaves

I can see the spirits
of yesterday
and they take me
by the hand
and they tell me
that the future holds golden statues
for me if I can just accept
the one thing we
all deny

I can be alone here on
this island for days and months
at a time and still
I feel surrounded
by all of the abuse and the
torment of a people who
gathered here centuries ago

to wait out
the rains of winter
and await
the coming of
the springtime fish
as they storm and attack
the river

I can swim in the river
outside my home and
go toward the sky
and I will still be all
alone as the words
of songs come to me
but I do not carry the
gift of songs
so the songs
keep going and
going

I can wait and wait
for love to grab
a hold of me
but I already lost her
to the darkness
of another man

and I remember that
day as I kicked in the door
with murder and mayhem
on my mind but I
did what I always do

I walked away alone
to this island
where there are centuries
of who I am
replayed over and over
again as I become
the torment
of myself

and no one cares
to comfort me in my
time of need

so I sit here
and I can see it all
as it becomes
a song but the words
are lost as I do
not have the
gift of song
and over
and over again
I am the torment
of myself
even if the spirits
told me so
I still
act
like
a human
and
deny

My confession

I must confess
the troubles of our people
still exist
but you learn to
mind your own business
and you take out your garbage
and you lock your doors
and you shut your windows

this is a reservation
like all the others
you can find along
this river of life and death
and I have seen both sides
of this double-edged sword

I have seen
fish in the thousands
and I have also
pulled bloated bodies
from the same waters

it is April
here in Kwantlen
and we are a people
who used to be able
to run for hours
and not get tired
and we are about 200
and although some of us
come from gods

there are people like me
who come from
a family that has
survived
for thousands of years

and now
my son
raises his gun
as there is trouble
down the road
as the bastards
still try
and take from us

take it you fools
as you
know not
what is really here

there are centuries
of spirits
ever ready to
defile you
you simple folk
who take and take
so now I give
to you
my confession:
forgive me lord
for I have
sinned

A sacred world

I have loved all the women
who called me on the phone
late at night when I
thought for sure I would
always be a loner

like a man
no longer needed
I was able
to fade into a
smoke-filled room where
all you could hear were
the songs from a place
we are not supposed
to go

the sacred stays sacred
and we are only given
glimpses of it
and we keep it forbidden
as it is not ours to share

the smoke falls to the night sky
of a winter
and you can still hear them
pounding the drums
as all the people
who belong there
rise up and hold their hands
up to the sky
and say thank you

I attempt to speak
but words are not mine
and it is a language
that once belonged
to my people
but like everything else
that we had
it is gone

so I stand up
and I attempt to speak
and when I cannot
I begin to cry
and this is who I am
and no one
but those who can hear me
will guide me around
the room in a haze
of smoke
and the temptation
of all that is sacred
falls to the cold night sky
of a world
so
so
sacred

We walk together

we have walked
beside each other
from the first days of our life
we step forward and this
is as long as we are able to

sometimes when you step
out on your own
you look back
and wait to see if
those who once walked with
you will appear

we walk so our young will follow
and sometimes we stumble
as those ahead of us
have stumbled
and we watch our young stumble
but we pick them up
and lead them to a better place

we walk into another spring day
but our hearts are heavy
as one of us
has stumbled
and has been taken
far too soon

we walk together
and remember
all of our loved ones
as they begin
their new walk
on the other side of the road
on the other side of the river
and they walk up the highest mountain
and sit
and watch us
as we
stumble
fall
get up
and move forward
into another
spring day
as the young
of this world
bow their heads
in memory
of their sister
taken
far too soon
from
all
of us

The rumour

I am the suicide of all that's lost
I am the suffering of the rumour
I am the politeness
given to a man
who never really
had much to say

there in the corner
sit all my empty bottles
stacked in a perpetual
monument
of forgiveness

I am the paper king of
a people who walked
and walked and when
they came to this river
they all dove in
and took one fish each
as if it was a gift
from a lost heaven

I am the poet who
never really had
much to say
and they will bury me
in a hole
and line the casket
with all of my poems
so I can eternally
relive the rumour

there on a hill sits a girl
and she is all alone
but she
begins to speak
and tells us that
she had found
all the lost women
and that they
are hungry

so we
the living lost
will burn food
for the lost
on the other side

I light the fire
and burn the plates of food
and every so often
I throw in one of my poems
for the lost to read
and they do
with a belly full of food
and I hear the laughter
of the lost
as they tell me
that I have yet to suffer
like the lost
I have
yet
to
suffer
the
rumour

The old days

a spider's used up web
the song of rain birds
the fallen West Coast rains
an echo of a song
a sleeping family
the cat cries for more food

the earth of a planet called Earth
swells up in the night
as another great child
is born into a world
where we are in need
of great people

all of us have become
so cold to the other that
when death comes
it is accepted
and it is never explained
like the old days

the flow of a torn ribbon
two apples given away in ceremony
a thank you card filled with lies
a bottle of hand sanitizer
and cherry flavoured candy

at once it comes together
in a perfect painting
painted by
a great person

one of a few still here
on the earth of a planet
called Earth

as the world
crumbles
and fades
there is hope
in the distance
as rain birds chirp
until
they become
a single chorus
of an old song
that is too old for us
to understand
so we accept it
because to deny
any of it would
mean we are done
and the cold world
we all have created
would become
a
used
up
spider's
web

Am I the one?

I could wake up
and destroy myself
completely
but I have to get up
and get the kids to school

there once was a boy
so beautiful
that
other
boys
and men
condemned
him

I am the fisherman
with gifts
and memories
that I throw
away
to the river

I took the meds
so my mind
will not turn
to a liquid
that will spill over
the edges
of
my madness

they told me that my
crooked teeth
would one day
fall out

they said the scars
around my eyes
would one day
turn to glorious
pieces of art

am I the one
for you?
am I the one you
will understand
and caress at night
as we both hold
the other
never wanting
to let go?

am I the one?

the broken
forgotten
original?

a man
so
forgotten
that I
had to ask:
am I the one?

Finding the animal

three black birds hop down
our dirt road
picking
at the road kill

the darkness of my room
reminds me of
the deep depression
that this poet
finds himself within

I have worn the same shoes
for over a year now
and one fits perfectly
and the other does not

cigarettes in hot July heat
taste like warm shit mixed with
a haunted feeling
of despair covered over
by a knowing of
what the fuck?

got boat and motor
ready to fish
but the world argues
about who gets the fish this year
and like everything else
given a dollar value
the river fish will
disappear

I see myself on a
dead river
eating road kill
as the three black birds
laugh and laugh
and I say to them go ahead
and laugh fuckers
and I will cry because for us
tears and sorrow
are the laughter
of the other side

the other side
where cigarettes
taste like a perfectly
slowly cooked fish
as the fatty juices
slip off and burn in the fire
placed there by someone
long before me
someone who knew
this day would come
as the three birds stop
and look at me
one more time
and then they take off
into a sky
given to us
yes
given
to
us

Where we are now

the epic poke of a needle
and that horizon paradise
as the east side engulfs
all of the rodents

an Indian man
and a paper bag
of memories
pukes
his golden life
onto the
sun-worn
hardened streets

this is 2018
in a place
where the humans
devour the humans
as if we created it all
for our gluttony

the streets join in the
middle as a woman
screams terrified by
the hold mankind has
on her as she slips into
a deep sleep
still
wearing
her best dress

where have they gone
our sisters?

where have they
disappeared to?

over there
across the
mountains
and the forests
of a time long before
our time

the women sit
and weave
the blankets
for the next one

but she defies it all
and fights back
sticking the blade
of treacherous steel
into the killer's heart
as his blood flows
to the streets
yes the streets
where rodents
become humans
and the feast
repeats
as if it was
Monday
July
2018

Smile looking down

inside of me
are the scars
of battles lost
to others who show
no scars or harm
done to them

outside of me
are the
scars
of battles lost
to others who kept
on coming

when I was four
I fell
and hit my head
and since then
I have nightmares
of falling down a hole
and trying to climb out
as my fingers slip
and I fall
forever

the women tell me
that my eyes hold
much beauty
and I tell them
over and over
that my eyes can see
the beauty in them

the women come and go
and I have had my share
of them all
and when
I was with them
I could not
smile looking down

there is this one woman
who has me now
and I try
and appear normal
but all the scars open
and my eyes are covered
by the moonlight
and I am only able
to smile at her
and move away so far
that the moonlight
can no longer cover me
as I walk towards
the big sleep
with tired eyes

I cover my face
with scarred hands
and it is then
I can see myself
at four years old
falling
with
my
smile
looking
down

The glorious rains

if Jesus was my
brother I would tell
him I am cold
so share some of
the blanket

if God was a gambling man
I would bluff
and go all in
and bet even my soul
if I ever had one

if eagles could
speak English
I am sure
they would tell us to
fuck off!

if trees fall
and they screamed at the end
of the fall it would
be heard by all the stars
in the sky
and they would clap
and stand in ovation

if only I had landed
the sweet punch
my face would
not look like someone
kicked the door
to my eyes

if the dragonfly
could drink beer
I am sure he would
have something important
to say like the rains
the rains
bring to us
glory

if the archangel Gabriel
could whisper to me
that I will find true love
I would burn my wings
and accept religion
for what it is worth

if my kids falter
I will pick them up
and put my life
up for auction
to protect them from the
long-tongued liar

if this day floated away
with me in it
I would say
hey, Jesus
pass the blanket
because
the rains
the rains
bring to us
our
glory

Passage to exhale

they say I come
from
a stone
placed here
by a doctor
who could
eat fire

there in the waters
they say are creatures
so beautiful that
a fisherman
with a broken heart
does not stand
a chance

up in the hills are
an army of little people
who quite enjoy
the company of fools
and demons both

out in the winds
of history
there were warriors
along the riverbanks
who waited for
outsiders and they would
club them
to death

today we welcome
everyone into our village
and then the carnage
begins

I have seen murder and waste
and all that goes with poverty
but the old church looks
so sweet with new
flowers all in row

this is the reservation called #6
of our people
the Kwantlen
and we accept our past
as the future glooms

I am on a
passage to exhale
as my body
turns once again
to stone
and I raise
my fists
in defiance
of those who
try
try
and try
to will me to the
back of the church
to kneel with the other
Kwantlen kids
as we sing a hymn

of a god who once
we waited for on the
riverbanks
to club him
but he never showed up
so we kneeled
on the river banks
like good children
made
of
stone

On the stage of life

the rules of
the game of love
for those who
wish to see you live
a good way

the taste of victory
having played the greatest game
this world could give us

the sweat and tears
of raising children
and wanting only
the best for them
and their
journey

the place where you go
when you die
and it's over
they're past all the bullshit
we go through
in our time
in this world
that when I was in love
with this girl
that it
was going to end
in tragedy
as we both
played the parts

on stage
in a play
written
for us

that my words will
live long in a book
shoved between the Bible
and the book of lies

that the plays I write
will give the stages
of this world passage
by the pile of shit
I have lived through

that I come from an ancient
people who have fished this
river for thousands of years

that this year
there are no fish
and they have been slowly
wiped out by the knowledge
and greed of my
oppressor

that when they took my mother
to a residential school
that I didn't stand a chance
but I showed them all
for one little Indian boy
with a pen in his hands
can destroy the past as if
it didn't happen at all

that one day I will
step out into this world
to the applause of the crowd
as I grace
this mighty stage
over there
past the pile shit
that we had to
call
life

Fire from the sky

in this heat
it makes
you want to
pull the
trigger
and say
fuck it

but you don't, no, you
drop some ice in a cup
and fill it with water and
you douse your suicide

I know, I know
my words are always
to do
with some despair
or the other but
fuck it
this is the mind they gave me
from the second-hand store

it's late on a July day
on the West Coast
of a planet probably too
close to the sun
and too close
to the fire in the sky
and I have to chop down a poem
in time and relive a moment
or even a lifetime

so this pen of black ink
scratches the lines of
an old notebook given to me
by someone who
tasted a poem or two
of mine

the sweat forms
and pours
down my arms
and I try
with all of my strength
to squeeze the pen so the
words of a prophet can
reach out to you, yes, you
my dear
my love
you are what creates the heat
in me and
you do not even know
I exist

when I see you in the
winter I melt away
to a corner
and sit quietly
with my drum
as the others
gather and sing
for their supper
and now in the burden
of yet another
record-breaking day
on Earth

you are all I can imagine
as black ink falls and moves
with my sweat of a heart
so filled with
love for you and if
you only knew
yes
if
you
only
knew

Late summer moon

these thoughts
of a general falseness
cover me up
when I pull the blanket
up close to my face
as the fan blows
cool air across the room

these pictures of my childhood
when I was beaten for what
I cannot recall
as the new kitten
bites at my feet
and I kick her away
and she comes back
and attacks my feet even
more as the hot air
of an August moon
fills the room
and I kick off the blanket
and the cat
stares at me
and smiles

these thoughts of a woman
in my bed
carry me
destroy me
devour me

as a song
comes on the radio
by Velvet Revolver
cutting the air
with the licks
of a guitar
and drums

as she goes into
an orgasmic bliss
screaming my name
which I have forgotten

even though they
told
me my name
when
I was little
but it was beaten
out of me
when I
was little

as I tried
to hide from the
lick of
a black leather belt
across my skinny ass
and she screams for me
to hold on
and we do
as she escapes
past the August moon

these thoughts of all
the liars of the world
who told me I
would overcome all
the joys and tears
of life and death
here
on this reservation
where women come
to my bed
and the kitten smiles
as the fan blows cool air
into the humid expressions
of the August moon
and another woman
takes me away
and we both let go
and then another woman
appears
and the blanket
covers us
as we both
sway in the sweat
and tears
as both of us
remember
a childhood
even though
it belonged
to
someone
else

Man of the madhouse

I am not
your everything
nor will I ever be that man
that takes you by the hand
and walks with you
into paradise

a very stable man
as the years of fights and punches
to my face and body
take their toll
and I do not bend properly
nor do I defend myself
like I did when I was
four years old
and took on
six white boys
beating them
with my hockey stick

full of pity
now I know enough
not to delve too much
into my own head because
all there is are moments
of frightening scenes of deceit
and false glory of a man
who does not even today
tie his shoes
no, he slips them on
like the slippers
of a man who

lives calmly
in a madhouse
on top of a hill
the boy with beauty in his eyes
as all the girls wanted a piece of him
but he faded back
to the sorrowful man
he is today
and we find him
all alone writing poems
about a past that was not
even his to begin with

no, I am the man
of many madhouses
let go
on a day
given enough meds
to appear normal
for a few moments
but then the meds
do not work and he
picks up his
hockey stick
and swings violently
at the air
at the past
at the horror
of a boy
who used
to
be
beautiful

A new chapter

the evolution of who I am
is now in its 5th chapter

50 years here inside
this skin of mine

I thought I did ok
as failure was always an option

the outside looking in should
be in my favour

I have not let myself
be the burden of another

why do we do that?

I have been in love
with all sorts
and they knew
from the first kiss
that I was the wrong
man

to hold you would have
been much better than
trying to hold on to you

I was a great drunk
with fists flying
at the drop
of a cold stare

I loved drugs
didn't we all?

but I was one
streetcar ride away
from the Hell
of the east side
of any city

all of this
I know is
pure shit for you
to read about

so I will walk on
into the spring
of the 6th chapter
of my life

this fucking life
so glorious
and tragic
will be the
death of me
as the epilogue
of a man
holding his arms
outward
trying
to
hold
on
to
it
all

A dream

bore the name
took my time
when I stepped
to the other side

sat still as the
old Indians came
into the light

and there he was:
my spirit
an old man
smoking a cigarette
as he began to sing
and dance around the
dirt floor

they say
dreams are real
and they are
if only I could
believe in them

I am not superstitious
and I know
the end will come
when it comes
and so
until then
I will believe
in my existence

this gift
this dream
of a life
given to me
fifty years ago
as I entered
into a room
and lit a cigarette
and I began to sing
and dance

old times
are the best
as new times
are a struggle
but it is a
good struggle

so I dream
and dream
and I believe in
who I have become:
an old man
who bores the name
of Joseph
not a saint
but a humble
old man
as
the
cigarette
burns

Beating the odds

I am the man that
lovers call when they need
to feel adored

I am the second choice
but that is ok
as I will devour you
until you beg me
to stop

I have been the hidden lover
and I have been the first choice
but some days you take
what she gives you
and sometimes all that
will be a quick look
in a crowded room

and down you go to her
and that is all that the
gamblers gave you:
a one hundred to one
shot in the dark

and not to say
I have not fallen
so to all my past lovers
I say to you that I have fallen
and as I get up
and as I break and replace the odds

I say to you
please write
please call
please take a quick look
in a crowded room
and I will fall to my knees
until you beg me away
as we replace the odds
one more time
so place your bets
on this man
who beat the odds
again
and
again

Perhaps

I should put my sunglasses on
I should dive deep into
the ocean and swim with
all my past lovers

I bet they never saw it coming

I know for a fact that
I have lived too long

there is a picture of me
somewhere

there will be peace on earth
though I doubt that
as another bomb
falls

there will be a write up
about how great a poet
I could've been

the lady across from me
knows who I was

the lady at the front desk
wasn't even
looking at me

the lady at the coffee shop
tells her friends
about me

the lady who betrayed me
will be famous
and on TV

I can't write worth shit
I can't even form a thought
I can't even die
as gracefully
as my old man

I might just keep walking
into this perfect picture
that some woman
has of me

perhaps
yes
perhaps

Acceptance

a bottle of water
a cold cup of joe
a broken pencil
the memory
of the hug of a good woman
and that you felt good
as if accepted

went into the city
and everyone was
breathing my air
so I split
and dodged the traffic
back into the valley
of soulless Indians
and they hugged me
and it felt good
as if I was accepted

set the table
and invited all of my
friends
and not one of them
showed up
and it was then
I knew how alone
I actually had become

Valentine's Day
and I will miss out
on all the joyous
escapades
of lovers
who tell the other
how much love they
have

I will wake up
light a smoke
dance out to the edge
of my world
and dance back
always listening
to that Johnny Cash song:
"God's gonna cut you down"
and it's as if I
will be hugged by
everything that
terrifies me,
can't you guys see it?
over there
past the hug
of
a
good
woman

Let us play

I am at a beggar's banquet
and all my little friends
are with us

we are here to pay our respect
to the one who got lost
on his way home
from the bar

we found him floating
in the river
and he was
cold and hungry
so we fed him
a plate of fish and rice
and we even gave him
a sip of beer
to warm him up

I am in a place
where all our whispers
come to get away

and if you listen
you can hear all
of your secrets
as they are
kept here
for eternity

and here the little ones
play a game of bones
as their whispers
become screams

as one side cheats
the other side

and you can still
hear the whisper of
decadence
as they dine upon
a plate of fish and rice

I am on a broken reservation
and we gather
and hurt
and blame
each other
as if that ever
solved
anything
and the little ones
do not come
and they stay
hidden
in the cedar trees
as the hungry people
of this reservation
blame each other

and we all sit down on the wet grass
overlooking the river
and we do not whisper
and we do not scream
as from the sky falls
eternal
plates
of
fish
and
rice

Darkness

been told I have
some mental problems

was a drunk by the age of 19
was a drug addict by the age of 26
I took some good beatings
early and late in life
and now my brain swims in a
mess of worry

torn bones
broken hands
a groin that aches
one good eye
I bite my tongue
every night
in a restless sleep

take the meds
as they are a part
of the routine

I sing and dance
when all my self-pity
explodes
onto a dirt floor

I know the teachings
I know the end
so I fight very day
looking for a
good man

but all I can see
with my one good eye
is a small boy
who never grew up

he just kind of
stopped
and became
an old man
who smokes way too much
who worries too much

mental illness
they called it
but I know
that one day
when all is done
I will breathe that
final breath
and close my one good eye
and I will swim beside
my brain
in
a
pool
of
tranquility

One day

a circle of lines on a book
with no name
a man cutting down a tree
with no leaves to speak of

I have sinned
I have been left behind
I have danced with the Devil
I have stolen a wife from a monster

a wanted poster on a post office wall
a pastime of smoke
and drink in a room

I will one day love you
I will lie for my supper
I will kick the habit
I will always love you

a rock becomes a rock
a wind becomes a story
a boat becomes our life
a moment in time fades

I am you
I am them
I am many
I am only a few

a church burns
a priest falls
a religion soars
a people follow the scars

I live in a hole
I dine on the breast of you
I kiss her as you kissed her
I fall from that hole

a part of me is a part of you
a city sleeps
a homeless man is at home
a drunk pours his last sip in memory

I've never been true
I've never been alive
I've never said I am sorry
I've never
forgotten
all
of
them

The director

eagles sit in a tree
in the rain
in the time
of all of us
where there will
be only happiness

over there
the old ones
sit quietly trying
to avoid living
near us

us
the mass
of beings
here and now
tossing the fortune
away because
we do not really
need it
in the river

the fish
wait for the worm
but it does not come
so the fish
sit there
beneath the rain
laughing at the eagles

as they sit there
in the rain
mumbling teachings
for us

us
the mass
here and now
the mass
of spoiled youth
we devour the world
in one final
gulp
yummy
it tastes like
long ago
but the old ones
want nothing to do with us
or the final taste

in my home
I have no friends
or love letters

all I have
is this lit cigarette
a cold cup of coffee
and the taste of an old
lover who walked away
and now all I have is
this final taste
and it is just for me

and this mass
of humans
can go to hell
because
this is the last meal
for me

as the rains pound
the eagles
and the fish watch
and dance across the universe
as all that is beautiful
appears before me

and the world awakes
to the calm morning
of peace on Earth
for you
and us
the mass
of this
whatever
it
was

I am my own memory

I saw her again
at a big gathering
as we were all there
to cry in the new year
as a thousand drummers
pounded deerskin drums
as the women cried and cried

she sat 10 rows up
with her group
her people
her tribe
and I hid underneath
in a hallway
away from all the hustle

I think our eyes met
but she just looked
right through me
past me
into the
end of me

and I backed up
and smothered myself
with all the self-pity
a grown man
could muster
and asked myself:
why do you do this?
why?

and the night tore on
and slowly
the crowd faded
and it was just my spirit
sitting there
in a big house
with the fires gone out
and the rains fell

happy new year
you big baby
next time take a longer
look at myself
and decide then and there
that one day at least
I would ask her
what her name was

one day
maybe next year
I will have grown up
and will have stopped this
everlasting mind from feeling
like I am no one
a loner
a child lost
without his mother
and next time
we cry in the new year
I will stand up
and walk up to her
and whisper:
I
really
love you
goodbye

A winter morning

wake the voices
in my head
the quiet world
has taken someone
way too soon

tragic end to
a good person
and the whole river and valley
of humans are
hurting

it's a cold December morning
and I know about death
and I know about life
but that does not make it
easier when a death
falls on all of us
and we accept
because you have to
accept and you have
to move on
and that is what we do
us
the indians
of a river
that feeds
all of us
and has for thousands
of years

this morning
warmed
by
a far away
sun
as the song birds
dance outside
my window
and I
like all
the river indians
we remember
our fallen

and we pick up
the pieces
and we move on
and we will feed
our lost lives
plates of fish
taken from the
river
that follows
all of us
on both sides
of life
and
death

Look at her

there she goes
the perfect
spirit
frees me

the way she walks
the way she smiles
even though she cries
out loud in her sleep

the demons
of before me
of before I even get there
they haunt her
they are her
they are

there she goes with her
past tucked beneath her pillow
as we
the river people
gather in a large room
of other winter river people

she doesn't even know
I exist
but I do
and I smile at her
and she looks away
far beyond me

and the night is over
and the gathering is over
and the guests leave
and they go home
and I get into my truck
and turn it on
and I drive down river
to the island
where I can disappear

and there she is
under my pillow
as my demons
haunt me
and I light a cigarette
and blow the smoke
up into the
black of sky

and there she goes
there she goes
again
in a dream
given to me
by another
spirit
who told me
that she is perfect
and that no one
can have her

but we try
don't we
as I smash
myself
into dust
as I try
over
and
over
just
to
look
at
her

The stone circle

I am not the lizard king
and with my tail
between my legs
I venture up river
to a place where
there is a tale about
a woman of the river
who will give
to me
eternal
life

I am not the king
of this lost kingdom
downriver
nor upriver
of all the
treacherous cities
of empty people
who breathe in
all the air
and breathe out
all the air
as the purpose
of being here was
worth all the forests
of the world

I am not the soldier of
a faith so golden
that within it

death is seen
as a greater step forward
than forgiveness
and acceptance

I am not the river warrior
put here as a stone
and told to share
all of my stories
with the young people so
they may carry on in
a good way

I am not the lover
of all lovers
and my empty bed
tells the truth
as year after year
I fall asleep alone
with no one to hold me
and to lie to me
and tell me that I will
one day
accept it
all

I am not the push to
push
all the rains of the sky
up there where
they throw stones
upon us and tell us
that we are not living

properly as we all destroy
this earth together
as the lizard king
as the soldiers and warriors
and all the lovers
gather in a circle
of stones
they grab a hold of me
and give to me
the hand
of a beautiful woman
from upriver
somewhere past
the creation
of who I am
as the push
is a
push

Living hell

been a year
since the fish filled my nets
and I could sit and count
the thirty pieces of silver given
to me from God

here, little Indian child
come to our schools
and cut your hair
and hide your tongue
and do not speak
because how could you
you savage
have anything
good to say
to the Lord

eat his body and drink
yes
of course
drink until
you turn into a fire beast of
anger and hatred and you destroy
yourself in some bar downtown
and you piss your pants
and wake up decades later
with a needle in your arm
and you sit there
crucified
asking
for forgiveness

yes do have children and we will
scoop them up and tear away
any religion created in a
cave and we will give them
only one book
for their lives
to read over again
as the fields of angels
sing songs of heaven and hell
and fire and flames

as the final candle in the
old rez church ignites the
gasoline poured there by
a little Indian boy who watches
the cross of the Lord burn
sending embers into
a cold night

you see me with my twisted face
beaten over again for standing
up and hiding in a world
where they want to reconcile
me but the wounds
they are too deep
and the pages
of that one book
flap and burn in a fire
lit a long time ago
as angels sing
of Heaven and Hell

as the Indian in me
throws a right and then a left
as the air of my punches
fan the fire
of
this
hellish
reservation

People trying to sleep

when I walk into the ocean
I am overwhelmed with all
that I have behind me

the years of thoughts
and experiences
that are soon washed away
and become a wave
as it hits the shore
and disappears

when I was a young man
I loved more than I was loved
and I slept with all the beauties
of this earth
and together
we created bliss and lust
and awkward love-making
and with it
ended I think
the words
I love you
fell off somewhere over there
past the city
in the desert

when I was mid-life
I was broken up into pieces
and each piece was given to a god
and those gods kept me
in their pockets

and the world for me
now is abandoned and forsaken
and I am one piece of
many pieces lost
in the pockets
of supposed gods
who never say to me:
we love you, man

as they bury me in a place
across the river from here
I close my eyes for one
last time and hear
the dirt being shovelled
and I feel the tears
of all the lovers who
were the only ones to show up
to bury this lover-poet
this pocket-god
as the last wave of who I was
disappears
into the sands
of a shoreline
over there
past the
city
in
the desert

Writing on the wall

the voices in my head keep
telling me to hurt myself
why?
I ask

I could never do it
too afraid of the carnage afterwards
and I have seen it
before when my grandfather
shot himself in the head when
I was fourteen
as he called his family
on the phone
and gave a drunken
goodbye

how could I out do such
a performance?

that is what it is
it would be my
final performance
and thank you for coming
please leave out the back door
and come again next time
I am in town

so the battle with the voices
the thoughts
the images
played over again and again